SCOOBY-DOO!

SPACE DISCOVERIES

INVESTIGATING THE MILKY WAY AND OTHER GALAXIES WITH VELMA

by Ailynn Collins

CAPSTONE PRESS
a capstone imprint

Published by Capstone Press, an imprint of Capstone
1710 Roe Crest Drive
North Mankato, Minnesota 56003
capstonepub.com

Library of Congress Cataloging-in-Publication Data
is available on the Library of Congress website.

ISBN: 9781669021384 (hardcover)
ISBN: 9781669021155 (paperback)
ISBN: 9781669021346 (ebook PDF)

Summary: When you gaze up at the night sky, all the stars you see are
part of our own Milky Way galaxy. The Milky Way holds 100 to 400
billion stars! Learn about how galaxies form, the perplexing mysteries of
black holes, and how galaxies can differ from one another with science
expert Velma and the rest of the Scooby-Doo gang.

Editorial Credits
Editor: Carrie Sheely; Designer: Elyse White;
Media Researcher: Rebekah Hubstenberger;
Production Specialist: Whitney Schaefer

Image and Design Credits
Alamy: Matteo Omied, 20 (top), Science History Images, 28-29, World
History Archive, 23 (bottom); Getty Images: Hulton Archive/Stringer,
16 (middle right), NASA/Handout, 10 (bottom right), Pakin Songmor,
1, 32, Ron Miller/Stocktrek Images, 13 (top), sololos, 8-9; NASA: ESA/
CSA/STScI, 24-25 (all), ESA/Hubble & NASA, D. J. Rosario, A. Barth/L.
Shatz, 18-19, JPL-Caltech, 14 (middle left), JPL/ESA/Herschel/PACS/
MESS Key Programme Supernova Remnant Team and Allison Loll/
Jeff Hester (Arizona State University), 10-11; Science Source: Mark
Garlick, 27 (middle); Shutterstock: Alex Mit, 2-3, 14-15 (background),
30-31, Aphelleon, front cover (bottom right), arvitalyaart, front
cover (background), Avigator Fortuner, 20-21 (background), BEST-
BACKGROUNDS, 19 (middle right), cddesign.co, design element
(planets), Denis Belitsky, 6-7, Jodi Cowan, front cover (middle left),
back cover (background), Klavdiya Krinichnaya, 22-23 (background),
Shark_749, 13 (background), solarseven, 4-5, sripfoto, 16-17
(background), Zakharchuk, 26-27 (background)

Table of Contents

Words in **bold** are in the glossary.

Our Marvelous Milky Way

Velma, Shaggy, Scooby, and the rest of the Mystery Inc. gang have finished setting up their tents. They are ready to enjoy their camping trip in a park. As darkness falls, they gaze up at the clear night sky.

The best time to see a sky full of stars is when it's super dark. We have to travel far away from cities too. The city lights make the stars harder to see. This spot is perfect!

The stars you see are part of our **galaxy**, the Milky Way. A galaxy is a giant collection of gas, dust, rocks, and stars held together by **gravity**.

FACT
Spring and fall are good times to look at the night sky. It is usually best around the new moon phase. During this time, the moon is less visible in the sky.

See that long streak of stars that has a milkiness to it? That's why it's called the Milky Way.

Cool! That reminds me, we're going to need milk for our cookies!

Long ago, there weren't **telescopes** to help people see distant objects in the sky. People couldn't see the individual stars in the Milky Way. It looked like a band of hazy light.

People came up with stories to explain this band. The ancient Greeks told of how the goddess Hera sprayed milk across the sky. The Chinese thought it was a river in heaven.

In Armenia, they believed that the god of fire and thunder stole straw from the king. He spilled it in the sky while he was running away.

After the invention of telescopes in the early 1600s, scientists saw millions of stars in the Milky Way. They realized that the Milky Way is our galaxy.

Astronomers are scientists who study space. They estimate that the universe has hundreds of billions of galaxies. As new telescopes make more discoveries, this estimate could change.

Our Solar System

Our home **planet** Earth and seven other planets **revolve** around the sun. Together with other space objects, they make up the solar system. Besides Earth, our solar system's planets are Mercury, Venus, Mars, Jupiter, Saturn, Uranus, and Neptune. Our solar system is a part of the Milky Way.

Chapter 1

What's in a Galaxy?

Most astronomers believe that the universe formed in a "big bang" about 13.8 billion years ago. According to this idea, the universe began as a very hot single point. It then began stretching very quickly. One hundred eighty million years later, galaxies began to form.

FACT
The Milky Way has a peanut-shaped bulge in its center.

Scientists think there could be between 100 and 400 billion stars in the Milky Way alone!

Space is filled with stars, planets, and many rocks. There are also clouds of dust and gas that swirl together in violent movements. Scientists believe these clouds crashed into others to form small galaxies. These galaxies then grew larger by crashing into more galaxies.

The Milky Way is between 100,000 and 200,000 light-years across. One light-year is 5.88 trillion miles (9.46 trillion kilometers). With today's spacecraft, it would take us 2 billion years or more to cross it.

At the center of a galaxy is an object with gravity so powerful that nothing can escape from it—not even light. This object is called a black hole. Black holes hold together all the **matter** in the galaxies around them. Matter is anything that has weight and takes up space.

The black hole in the middle of the Milky Way is called Sagittarius A* (sa-juh-TAYR-ee-us AY-star) or Sgr A* (SADGE AY-star). It is a supermassive black hole. This is the biggest kind of black hole that modern scientists have studied. Sgr A* is 32.2 million miles (51.8 million km) across.

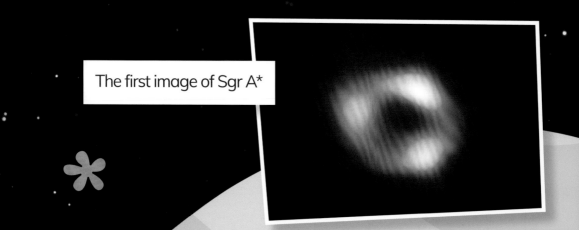

The first image of Sgr A*

When a star explodes, it sends its matter, dust, and gases back into the galaxy to make new stars. It's like cosmic recycling!

A supernova remnant left behind from a star explosion

There are millions of smaller black holes all over the Milky Way. Many form when a star dies. It uses up all its fuel and collapses or explodes.

In May 2022, astronomers were able to get a picture of the Milky Way's supermassive black hole for the first time. It will help them study how black holes form and grow.

Chapter 2

Galaxies of All Shapes

The Milky Way is a spiral galaxy. It looks like a huge, flat disk with arms that reach outward. Most galaxies scientists have discovered are spiral in shape.

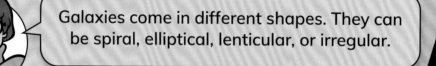
Galaxies come in different shapes. They can be spiral, elliptical, lenticular, or irregular.

Spiral?

Yeah, like how a cinnamon roll looks, Scoob.

Yum!

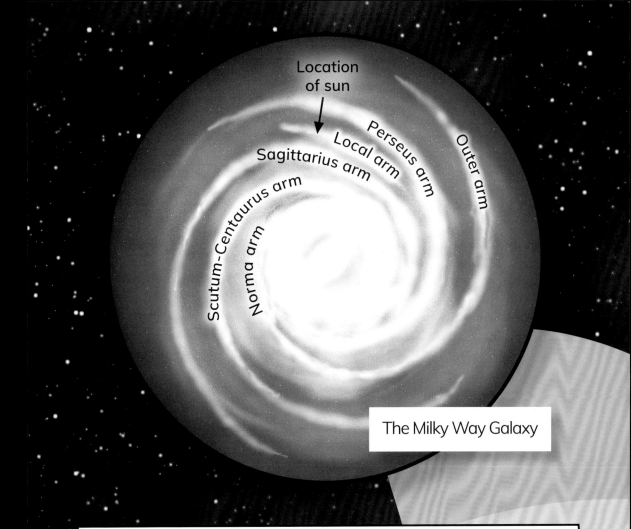

Location of sun

Perseus arm

Outer arm

Local arm

Sagittarius arm

Scutum-Centaurus arm

Norma arm

The Milky Way Galaxy

Scientists separate the Milky Way's arms into major and minor arms. The two major arms are named Scutum-Centaurus, or Scutum-Crux, and Perseus. These contain new and old stars. The two minor arms are called Norma and Sagittarius. They contain mostly gas and dust. Our solar system is in the Local arm, also called the Orion arm. It is between the Sagittarius and Perseus arms.

Elliptical galaxies look like stretched out circles. They can hold up to a trillion stars. Smaller ones are called dwarf elliptical galaxies. Elliptical galaxies are made up of older stars. They don't have much gas and dust.

A lenticular galaxy looks like the lens of an eye. One example is the Cartwheel Galaxy. It has an inner ring and an outer ring. The outer ring has several billion new stars.

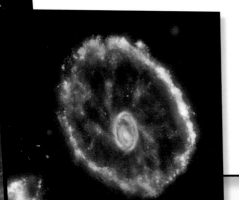

The Cartwheel Galaxy

Galaxies don't stay still. They travel through the universe. The Milky Way travels at 1.3 million miles per hour!

Galaxies

Galaxies that don't follow any shape are called irregular galaxies. They have no real shape but are affected by the gravity from their neighboring galaxies.

In 2015, **NASA's** Hubble Space Telescope took a photo of a dwarf irregular galaxy. It was called UGC 8201. Scientists saw many new stars. Because this galaxy is so close to the Milky Way, it's perfect for scientists to study how dwarf galaxies grow.

A New Galaxy Named

While growing up in Turkey, Burçin Mutlu-Pakdil loved looking at the stars. She went on to study the science of physics. Later, she moved to the United States to continue studying the universe. In 2016, she and her team discovered and began studying a new type of double-ringed galaxy. Some parts of the galaxy are older than others. It was named Burçin's Galaxy after her.

Chapter 3

Studying Galaxies

The knowledge scientists have about galaxies today is built upon the work of earlier scientists. Galileo Galilei was an astronomer who lived in the 1600s. In 1610, using his simple telescope, he saw that the Milky Way was made up of countless stars.

Galilei looks through a telescope at the night sky.

Back then, people believed that all the stars in the universe were inside the Milky Way. In 1923, astronomer Edwin Hubble started studying stars and their distances from Earth.

He discovered that some stars were too far away to be in the Milky Way. That's when he realized that there were more galaxies out there.

In the 1930s, Helen Sawyer Hogg studied star clusters. Her work gave scientists a way to estimate the age of our galaxy. It also helped scientists understand how galaxies form and grow.

When Galilei was alive, most people believed that Earth was the center of the universe.

Like, weird!

It may seem that way now. But back then, they didn't have the telescopes like we do today. The observations Galilei made led him to believe that the sun was the center of our solar system.

The Hubble telescope has been traveling in space for more than 30 years. In this time, it has taken more than 1.5 million photos. In 2022, Hubble showed us another spiral galaxy 110 million light-years away. It is known as NGC 7172. The black hole in the galaxy's middle was very bright, but it was hidden behind threads of dust.

The dark dust in front of NGC 7172's middle

NASA launched the James Webb Space Telescope in 2021. It's the most powerful space telescope ever built. It will be able to see objects farther than anything humans have seen before.

The primary mirror of the James Webb telescope has gold plating to help reflect light.

The James Webb telescope is 100 times more powerful than the Hubble telescope.

Telescopes in Chile that make up part of the Event Horizon Telescope stand on the ground with the Milky Way above.

Giant telescopes that are placed on land to study space are called ground-based observatories. They are placed away from cities. You can recognize most observatories by their dome shape.

A dome shape? Like a giant scoop of ice cream?

That's exactly right, Shaggy!

When one of these telescopes is in use, a window in the dome opens. It can rotate in every direction to get the best look at the galaxy. There are observatories in Hawaii, Chile, the South Pole, and other places.

In May 2022, scientists used eight giant telescopes working together to get the clearest image ever of Sgr A*. These telescopes make up the Event Horizon Telescope. They are placed all around the world. Their photos show us that the **mass** of Sgr A* is more than 4 million times the mass of our sun.

Jinkies! That's big!

Chapter 4

Dark Matter and Energy

Over many years, scientists have discovered that 27 percent of the universe is made up of something called dark matter. And it's invisible! How do we know it really exists?

Astronomers noticed that stars and galaxies swirl very quickly through the universe. These zooming galaxies should have been flung far into space. The spinning stars should have been torn apart. Instead, everything stays in position and in one piece.

Something with strong gravity is holding them all together in place. It could only be dark matter. But even today, scientists still don't really know what makes up dark matter.

It sounds like we have a mystery on our hands!

Yes, scientists are detectives just like us. They have set up equipment to try to detect dark matter. Some of the gear is underground.

Scientists use images of galaxy clusters to try to map where dark matter might be. In this image, scientists think dark matter is appearing as an outer ring.

And there's dark energy too! It makes up about 68 percent of the universe.

Scientists know that the universe has been getting bigger. They can measure how far other galaxies are from the Milky Way. That's how they know the universe is expanding. They think that dark energy might work like an opposite force to gravity. Scientists are still learning more about how dark energy works. In the meantime, dark matter and dark energy remain a mystery.

Just like the mystery of why Shaggy and Scoob are always so hungry!

Speaking of being hungry, where did the marshmallows go?

Traveling Back Through Time

The James Webb telescope can see stars that are very far away. The light from these stars travels far through space. The advanced telescope may even be able to "see" the first stars in the universe. This would be like traveling back in time. It could help scientists learn about how the universe was made.

Stephan's Quintet five-galaxy grouping from the James Webb telescope

A young, star-forming area in the Milky Way captured by the James Webb telescope is called Cosmic Cliffs.

Chapter 5

Our Galactic Neighborhood

Our galaxy has neighbors. The neighborhood is called the Local Group. It's made up of 50 galaxies. Most of these are smaller dwarf ones made up of a few billion stars. Our closest large neighboring galaxy is Andromeda. It's also the largest galaxy in the Local Group.

In the night sky, Andromeda is the most distant object that can be seen with the naked eye. The best time to see it is in the fall or winter from the Northern **Hemisphere**.

Andromeda has about 1 trillion stars. It's 2.5 million light-years from Earth. It would take us about 4 billion years to travel there.

Whoa! 4 billion years? Can't we get there faster?

Not yet. But scientists are always looking for ways to improve spacecraft technology.

Artwork shows some galaxies of the Local Group. The Milky Way is at the top left, Andromeda is at center-right, and Triangulum is at bottom right.

FACT

Persian astronomer Abd al-Rahman al-Sufi first discovered Andromeda in the year 964. He described it as a "small cloud."

The Large Magellanic Cloud (LMC) and Small Magellanic Cloud (SMC) are two irregular dwarf galaxies in our Local Group. They can be seen only from the Southern Hemisphere. They seem to be passing by our Milky Way instead of orbiting it.

These two galaxies contain more stars than other small galaxies. They're full of new stars being born. Scientists estimate that the SMC has about 3 billion stars. The LMC may contain 30 billion stars.

The LMC has many bright stars.

The giant Tarantula **Nebula** is a gas and dust cloud inside the LMC. Scientists think that this nebula is made of the remains of a large explosion that happened when a star died. It is the most active star-forming area in the Local Group.

This view is amazing! And it's just a very tiny piece of what our galaxy holds. We can only imagine what new discoveries will be made in the future!

Glossary

astronomer (uh-STRAH-nuh-muhr)—a scientist who studies stars, planets, and other objects in space

galaxy (GAL-uhk-see)—a very large group of stars and planets

gravity (GRAV-uh-tee)—a force that pulls objects with mass together

hemisphere (HEM-uhss-fihr)—one half of Earth; the equator divides Earth into northern and southern hemispheres

mass (MASS)—the amount of physical matter an object contains

matter (MAT-ur)—everything that contains atoms and takes up space

NASA (NAS-uh)—the abbreviation for the space agency of the United States, the National Aeronautics and Space Administration

nebula (NE-byu-luh)—a huge, bright cloud of gas and dust found in space

planet (PLAN-it)—a large object that moves around a star; Earth is a planet

revolve (ri-VOLV)—to keep turning in a circle or orbit around a central point or object

telescope (TEL-uh-skope)—a tool people use to look at objects in space; telescopes make objects in space look closer than they really are

Read More

Hulick, Kathryn. *The Night Sky*. North Mankato, MN: Abdo Publishing, 2022.

Lowery, Mike. *Everything Awesome About Space and Other Galactic Facts!* New York: Orchard Books, 2021.

Marinov, Isabelle. *The Boy Whose Head Was Filled with Stars: A Life of Edwin Hubble*. Brooklyn, NY: Enchanted Lion Books, 2021.

Internet Sites

Kiddle: Space Facts for Kids
kids.kiddle.co/Space

NASA Kids' Club
nasa.gov/kidsclub/text/index.html

Space.com
space.com

Index

About the Author

Ailynn Collins has written many books for children. Science and space are among her favorite subjects. She has an MFA in writing for Children and Young Adults from Hamline University and has spent many years as a teacher. She lives outside Seattle with her family and five dogs.